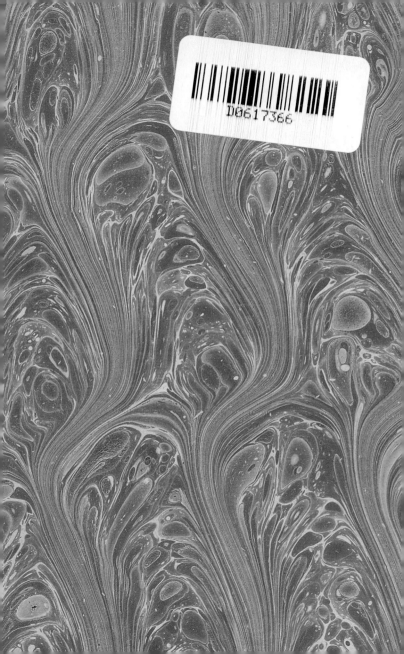
D0617366

Memories of Childhood

Memories of Childhood

BY
BARBARA MILO OHRBACH

*Old-fashioned
rhymes, poems, recipes,
and songs*

 CLARKSON N. POTTER, INC./PUBLISHERS
DISTRIBUTED BY CROWN PUBLISHERS, INC., NEW YORK

Every effort has been made to locate the copyright holders of materials used in this book. Should there be any omissions or errors, we apologize and shall be pleased to make the appropriate acknowledgments in future editions.

"Dogs," from *Around and About* by Marchette Chute. Copyright © 1957 by Marchette Chute. Reprinted by permission of the author. • "Everybody Says" and "Little," from *Everything and Anything* by Dorothy Aldis. Copyright 1925, 1927, copyright renewed 1953, 1955 by Dorothy Aldis. Reprinted by permission of G.P. Putnam's Sons. • "Little Brother's Secret," from *Poems* by Katherine Mansfield. Copyright 1924 by Alfred A. Knopf, Inc., copyright renewed 1952 by J. Middleton Murry. Used by permission of Alfred A. Knopf, Inc. • "Animal Crackers," from *Chimneysmoke* by Christopher Morley. Copyright 1917, 1945 by Christopher Morley. Reprinted by permission of Harper & Row, Publishers, Inc. • "The Birthday Child" by Rose Fyleman. Reprinted by permission of The Society of Authors as the literary representative of the estate of Rose Fyleman.

Published by Clarkson N. Potter, Inc., 225 Park Avenue South, New York, New York 10003, and represented in Canada by the Canadian MANDA Group

CLARKSON N. POTTER, POTTER, and colophon are trademarks of Clarkson N. Potter, Inc.

Manufactured in Japan

Design by Justine Strasberg

Library of Congress Cataloging-in-Publication Data

Ohrbach, Barbara Milo.
Memories of childhood.

1. Nursery rhymes.   2. Children's poetry.
[1. Nursery rhymes   2. Games]   I. Title.
PZ8.3.O36Me   1988   398'.8   88-17982
ISBN 0-517-57021-1
10 9 8 7 6 5 4 3 2 1

First Edition

To my nieces and nephews—
who fill our lives with love and laughter

A big thank you to everybody who worked on this little book with me. Their caring efforts made all the difference, especially—

Everyone at Clarkson N. Potter for their hard work and dedication.

Tina Strasberg for taking my memories and designing an enchanting book around them.

Beth Allen and her mother, Elva Allen; Gayle Benderoff; Lisa Fresne and her grandmother Betty Gunter; Deborah Geltman; Nancy and little Katie Greene; Patti McCarthy; and Gloria Schaaf for their good ideas.

And thank you to those people who for centuries have been creating and passing along the charming rhymes, fairy tales, fables, and poems that make up such a treasured part of all our childhood memories.

Introduction

T*he scenes of childhood are the memories of future years."*

I came across this quote in an old *Farmers Almanac* for 1850 and it seems to be as true now as it must have been then. Childhood, after all, is a very special time—safe, serene, and filled with wonder. And so much of what we remember and cherish about our early years stays with us forever.

When I was a young child, the highlight of the day was when my father came home from work and read to us before we reluctantly had to go to sleep. The simple rhymes and stories became old friends and we loved to hear them over and over—again and again. Our *Golden Books*, filled with favorites, always ended up dog-eared and worn-out. There is a photograph in one of our family albums of my sister and me, ages three and five. We are sitting in an old wing chair, wearing identical plaid

dresses, avidly "reading" our favorite
Mother Goose book.

Many years after that picture was
taken, I found myself reading the same
verses and singing the same lullabyes to my
dear nieces and nephews. Tucked in bed,
faces scrubbed and shiny, their blankets
pulled up high so that only their big, round
eyes showed, they would ask me to read just
one more rhyme—"just one, please, then
we *promise* we'll go to sleep!" Isn't it nice to
know that although everything seems to
change, some things never do. And that
these children of today are as enchanted
and captivated as we were by the same
centuries-old stories.

This short poem from a Victorian
child's picture book puts it sweetly:

The children in the fields at play,
They pluck the flowers that grow;
We used to pluck the self-same flowers
'A many years ago.

We love to watch the children's game,
Their troubles and their joys,
For did we not the very same
When we were girls and boys.

Children's literature is part of a tradition that goes back to the fables of the fourth century. The first children's book was printed in France in 1487 and Mother Goose first appeared in 1695. Many of their timeless messages are still with us and seem more meaningful than ever.

This little book is filled with many of my favorites, especially the most classic and familiar. It is illustrated with hand-colored engravings from old children's books collected over the years. I've had a wonderful time putting it together and remembering. As you read it to a child you love, I hope you enjoy remembering too.

Barbara Milo Ohrbach
New York City

HAPPY THOUGHT

The world is so full of a number of things,
I'm sure we should all be as happy as kings.

ROBERT LOUIS STEVENSON

I'M GLAD

I'm glad the sky is painted blue,
 And the earth is painted green,
With such a lot of nice fresh air
 All sandwiched in between.

Little girl, little girl,
	Where have you been?
I've been to see grandmother
	Over the green.
What did she give you?
	Milk in a can.
What did you say for it?
	Thank you, Grandam.

Nana's Lemon Dreams

Lisa's grandmother has a wonderful daily ritual. Each afternoon she serves tea. Children, grandchildren, and now great-grandchildren are always included. Out comes the old pink luster teapot and, if you are lucky, that day there will be Nana's Lemon Dreams.

1 CUP FLOUR
1 TEASPOON BAKING POWDER
¼ TEASPOON SALT
½ CUP UNSALTED BUTTER
½ CUP SUGAR
2 EGGS, SEPARATED

3 TABLESPOONS LEMON JUICE
2 TABLESPOONS GRATED LEMON RIND
½ TEASPOON CONFECTIONERS' SUGAR
½ TEASPOON CINNAMON

✦ Preheat oven to 350°F. Lightly grease miniature muffin tins. Sift flour, baking powder, and salt in a bowl.

✦ Using an electric mixer, cream butter with sugar until fluffy. Add to flour mixture.

✦ Beat egg yolks one at a time and add to the bowl, alternating with the lemon juice.

✦ Beat egg whites until stiff. Then fold into batter with the lemon rind.

✦ Fill muffin tins ¾ full. Sprinkle with confectioners' sugar. Add cinnamon. Bake 25 minutes and let cool in tins.

MAKES ABOUT 24 MINIATURE MUFFINS

Little Bo-peep has lost her sheep,
And can't tell where to find them;
Leave them alone, and they'll come home,
And bring their tails behind them.

Peter Piper picked a peck of pickled peppers;
A peck of pickled peppers Peter Piper picked;
If Peter Piper picked a peck of pickled peppers,
Where's the peck of pickled peppers Peter Piper
picked?

Rub-a-dub-dub,
Three men in a tub,
And who do you think they be?
The butcher, the baker,
The candlestick-maker;
Turn 'em out, knaves all three!

Hey! diddle, diddle,
The cat and the fiddle,
The cow jumped over the moon;
The little dog laughed
To see such sport,
While the dish ran after the spoon.

Little Jack Horner
Sat in the corner,
Eating a Christmas pie;
He put in his thumb,
And pulled out a plum,
And said, What a good boy am I!

The Queen of Hearts
She made some tarts,
All on a summer's day;
The Knave of Hearts
He stole those tarts,
And took them clean away.

The King of Hearts
Called for the tarts,
And beat the Knave full sore;
The Knave of Hearts
Brought back the tarts,
And vowed he's steal no more.

It's raining, it's pouring,
The old man's snoring;
He got into bed
And bumped his head
And couldn't get up in the morning.

Cuckoo, cuckoo, cherry tree,
Catch a bird, and give it me;
Let the tree be high or low,
Let it hail or rain or snow.

WHAT ARE LITTLE BOYS MADE OF?

What are little boys made of, made of?
What are little boys made of?
    Frogs and snails
    And puppy-dogs' tails,
    That's what little boys are made of.

What are little girls made of, made of?
What are little girls made of?
    Sugar and spice
    And all things nice,
That's what little girls are made of.

What are young men made of, made of?
What are young men made of?
    Sighs and leers
    And crocodile tears,
    That's what young men are made of.

What are young women made of, made of?
What are young women made of?
    Ribbons and laces
    And sweet pretty faces,
That's what young women are made of.

NUMBERS

1, 2,
Buckle my shoe;

Three, four,
Knock at the door;

Five, six,
Pick up sticks;

Seven, eight,
Lay them straight;

9, 10,
A big fat hen;

Eleven, twelve,
Dig and delve;

13, 14,
Maids a-courting;

Fifteen, sixteen,
Maids in the kitchen;

Seventeen, eighteen,
Maids in waiting;

19, 20,
My plate's empty.

ONE AND ONE

Two little girls are better than one,
Two little boys can double the fun,
Two little birds can build a fine nest,
Two little arms can love mother best.
Two little ponies must go to a span,
Two little pockets has my little man;
Two little eyes to open and close,
Two little ears and one little nose,
Two little elbows, dimpled and sweet,
Two little shoes on two little feet,
Two little lips and one little chin,
Two little cheeks with a rose shut in;
Two little shoulders, chubby and strong,
Two little legs running all day long.
Two little prayers does my darling say,
Twice does he kneel by my side each day,
Two little folded hands, soft and brown,
Two little eyelids cast meekly down,
And two little angels guard him in bed,
"One at the foot, and one at the head."

MARY MAPES DODGE

Ickle ockle, blue bockle,
Fishes in the sea,
If you want a pretty maid,
Please choose me.

Patti's Macaroons

*W*hy do I associate
*macaroons with childhood? I don't know, but
most people I asked did too and remember them
with fondness. My good friend Patti, who is a
terrific cook, has a recipe that her mother loved.
Share these treats with a favorite child you know.*

⅓ CUP FLOUR
2½ CUPS SHREDDED COCONUT
    DASH OF SALT

⅔ CUP SWEETENED
   CONDENSED MILK
1 TEASPOON VANILLA

✦ Preheat oven to 250° F. and grease a cookie sheet well.

✦ Mix flour, coconut, and salt together in a bowl.

✦ Blend in the milk and vanilla. Stir well.

✦ Drop 2 tablespoons of the mixture at a time onto a cookie sheet. Leave 1 inch of space between each macaroon.

✦ Bake for 20 minutes until golden brown.

✦ Remove from cookie sheet immediately and cool on racks.

MAKES 15 TO 18 MACAROONS

Here is the church, and here is the steeple;
Open the door and here are the people.
Here is the parson going upstairs,
And here he is a-saying his prayers.

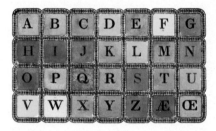

A.B.C.

A, b, c, d, e, f, g;
H, i, j, k, l, m, n, o, p;
Q, r, s, t, u, v;
W . . . x and y and z.
Now I've said my A. B. C.
Tell me what you think of me.

Hickory, dickory, dock,
The mouse ran up the clock.
The clock struck one,
The mouse ran down,
Hickory, dickory, dock.

12

Pat-a-cake, pat-a-cake, baker's man,
Bake me a cake as fast as you can;
Pat it and prick it, and mark it with T,
Put it in the oven for Tommy and me.

One potato, two potato,
Three potato, four;
Five potato, six potato,
Seven potato, MORE.

ROMAN FIGURES

X shall stand for playmates Ten;
V for Five stout stalwart men;
I for One, as I'm alive;
C for Hundred, and D for Five;
M for a Thousand soldiers true,
and L for Fifty, I'll tell you.

This little pig went to market;
This little pig stayed at home;
This little pig got roast beef;
This little pig got none;
This little pig cried wee, wee, all the way home.

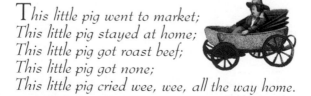

13

Sing a song of winter,
 Of frosty clouds in air!
Sing a song of snowflakes
 Falling everywhere.

NORMAN C. SCHLICHTER

THE LAND OF
COUNTERPANE

When I was sick and lay a-bed,
I had two pillows at my head,
And all my toys beside me lay
To keep me happy all the day.

And sometimes for an hour or so
I watched my leaden soldiers go,
With different uniforms and drills,
Among the bed-clothes, through the hills;

And sometimes sent my ships in fleets
All up and down among the sheets;
Or brought my trees and houses out,
And planted cities all about.

I was the giant great and still
That sits upon the pillow-hill,
And sees before him, dale and plain,
The pleasant land of counterpane.

ROBERT LOUIS STEVENSON

15

Thirty days hath September,
April, June, and November;
All the rest have thirty-one,
Excepting February alone,
And that has twenty-eight days clear
And twenty-nine in each leap year.

Spring is showery, flowery, bowery;
Summer is hoppy, croppy, poppy;
Autumn is wheezy, sneezy, freezy;
Winter is slippy, drippy, nippy.

THE STAR

Twinkle, twinkle, little star,
How I wonder what you are,
Up above the world so high,
Like a diamond in the sky.

When the blazing sun is set,
And the grass with dew is wet,
Then you show your little light,
Twinkle, twinkle, all the night.

Then the traveler in the dark
Thanks you for your tiny spark,
He could not see where to go
If you did not twinkle so.

In the dark blue sky you keep,
And often through my curtains peep,
For you never shut your eye
Till the sun is in the sky.

As your bright and tiny spark
Lights the traveler in the dark,
Though I know not what you are,
Twinkle, twinkle, little star.

JANE TAYLOR

17

We'll talk of sunshine and of song,
And summer days when we were young;
Sweet childish days that were as long
As twenty days are now.

WILLIAM WORDSWORTH

Aunt Barb's Brownies

Most children love brownies. Our nieces and nephews enthusiastically helped me to bake them when they were very little and even now, one of them always volunteers. Could it be because whoever helps gets to lick the spoon?

⅓ CUP UNSALTED BUTTER
¾ CUP SUGAR
2 TABLESPOONS WATER
2 CUPS SEMI-SWEET CHOCOLATE BITS

1 TEASPOON VANILLA
2 EGGS
¼ CUP UNSIFTED FLOUR
¼ TEASPOON BAKING SODA

✦ Preheat oven to 325° F. Grease a 9-inch square cake pan.

✦ Combine butter, sugar, and water and bring to a boil. Remove from heat. Add 1 cup of chocolate bits and vanilla. Stir until chocolate is melted and smooth.

✦ Add eggs, one at a time, stirring well.

✦ In a bowl, combine flour and baking soda. Gradually blend into chocolate mixture.

✦ Stir in remaining cup of chocolate bits.

✦ Spread into the pan and bake for 35 minutes. Cut into small squares when completely cooled.

MAKES ABOUT 24 SQUARES

Pease-pudding hot,
Pease-pudding cold,
Pease-pudding in the pot,
Nine days old.
Some like it hot,
Some like it cold,
Some like it in the pot,
Nine days old.

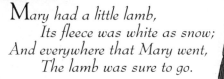

Mary had a little lamb,
Its fleece was white as snow;
And everywhere that Mary went,
The lamb was sure to go.

He followed her to school one day,
Which was against the rule;
It made the children laugh and play
To see a lamb at school.

Little Miss Muffet
Sat on a tuffet,
Eating of curds and whey;
There came a great spider
And sat down beside her,
Which frightened Miss Muffet away.

Humpty Dumpty sat on a wall,
Humpty Dumpty had a great fall;
Not all the king's horses, nor all the king's
     men,
Could set Humpty Dumpty up again.

Jack be nimble,
     Jack be quick,
Jack jump over
     The candlestick.

Little girl, little girl,
Where have you been?
Gathering roses to
     give to the queen.

Jack and Jill went up the hill,
     To fetch a pail of water;
Jack fell down and broke his crown,
     And Jill came tumbling after.

Bring the comb and play upon it!
Marching, here we come!
Willie cocks his highland bonnet,
Johnnie beats the drum.

ROBERT LOUIS STEVENSON

YANKEE DOODLE

Yankee Doodle went to town upon a little
pony,
He stuck a feather in his hat and called it
macaroni.
Yankee Doodle keep it up, Yankee Doodle
dandy,
Mind the music and the step, and with the
girls be handy.

LONDON BRIDGE

London Bridge is falling down, falling down,
falling down;
London Bridge is falling down, My Fair Lady.

23

Little Boy Blue, come blow your horn,
The sheep's in the meadow, the cow's in the
     corn;
But where is the boy that looks after the sheep?
He's under a hay-cock, fast asleep.
Will you awake him? No, not I;
For if I do, he'll be sure to cry.

Star light, star bright,
First star I see tonight,
I wish I may, I wish I might,
Have the wish I wish tonight.

Mistress Mary, quite contrary,
How does your garden grow?
With cockle-shells, and silver bells,
And pretty maids all in a row.

24

Old King Cole
  Was a merry old soul,
And a merry old soul was he;
  He called for his pipe,
    And he called for his bowl,
And he called for his fiddlers three.

Every fiddler he had a fiddle,
And a very fine fiddle had he;
    Oh, there's none so rare
    As can compare
With King Cole and his fiddlers three.

Georgie Porgie, pudding and pie,
Kissed the girls and made them cry;
When the boys came out to play,
Georgie Porgie ran away.

Baa, baa, black sheep, have you any wool?
Yes, sir; yes, sir, three bags full.
One for my master, one for my dame,
And one for the little boy that lives in the lane.

Ring-a-ring o' roses,
A pocket full of posies,
 A-tishoo! A-tishoo!
We all fall down.

Beth's Birthday Cupcakes

W*hen my friend Beth was a little girl, her mother always made delicious cupcakes for Beth's birthday. Topped with the pink parfait frosting, on page 31, and colored sprinkles, they made a special day even more special.*

1 CUP UNSALTED BUTTER
2½ CUPS SUGAR
5 LARGE EGGS
1 TABLESPOON VANILLA
2½ CUPS FLOUR
½ TEASPOON SALT

¼ TEASPOON BAKING SODA
1 CUP SOUR CREAM
1 TABLESPOON FINELY GRATED LEMON RIND

✦ Preheat oven to 325° F. Place paper liners in 24 muffin cups.

✦ Using an electric mixer, cream butter and sugar until fluffy.

✦ Gradually beat in eggs, two at a time, beating well after each addition. Add vanilla and beat two minutes more.

✦ Sift together flour, salt, and baking soda. Stir in flour mixture and sour cream. Add lemon rind. Fill muffin cups half full.

✦ Bake 20 to 25 minutes. Cool in pans 10 minutes. Remove from pan and cool completely.

MAKES 24 CUPCAKES

LITTLE BROTHER'S SECRET

When my birthday was coming
Little Brother had a secret:
He kept it for days and days
And just hummed a little tune when I asked
    him.

But one night it rained
And I woke up and heard him crying:
Then he told me.
"I planted two lumps of sugar in your garden
Because you love it so frightfully.
I thought there would be a whole sugar tree for
    your birthday.
And now it will all be melted."
O the darling!

KATHERINE MANSFIELD

THE BIRTHDAY CHILD

Everything's been different
    All the day long,
Lovely things are happened,
    Nothing has gone wrong.

Nobody has scolded me,
    Everyone has smiled.
Isn't it delicious
    To be a birthday child?

ROSE FYLEMAN

EVERYBODY SAYS

Everybody says
I look just like my mother.
Everybody says
I'm the image of Aunt Bee.
Everybody says
My nose is like my father's,
But I want to look like me.

DOROTHY ALDIS

Here we go round the mulberry bush,
    The mulberry bush, the mulberry bush:
Here we go round the mulberry bush,
    On a cold frosty morning!

This is the way we wash our clothes,
    Wash our clothes, wash our clothes:
This is the way we wash our clothes,
    On a cold frosty morning!

This is the way we clean our rooms,
    Clean our rooms, clean our rooms:
This is the way we clean our rooms,
    On a cold frosty morning!

Blind man, blind man, sure you can't see?
Turn around three times, and try to catch me.
Turn east, turn west, catch as you can.
Did you think you'd caught me?

Pink Parfait Frosting

This delightful frosting goes perfectly with Beth's Birthday Cupcakes on page 27. A nice birthday idea is to put out small bowls of different toppings: flaked coconut, M&M's, miniature marshmallows, gumdrops, or chopped nuts and let the children decorate their own.

1 CUP UNSALTED BUTTER, COLD AND FIRM
4 CUPS SIFTED CONFECTIONERS' SUGAR
1 TABLESPOON VANILLA

3 to 4 TABLESPOONS HEAVY CREAM
RED FOOD COLORING

✦ Beat butter in a small bowl until creamy and light yellow in color.

✦ Add sugar in 3 additions, beating well after each.

✦ Beat in vanilla, then just enough cream to reach medium spreading consistency. (Icing should hold ½-inch peak when dipped up with spatula.)

✦ Tint light pink with 1 to 2 drops red food coloring. Swirl with spoon onto cooled cupcakes and top each as desired.

Hearts, like doors, will ope with ease
To very, very little keys,
And don't forget that two of these
Are "I thank you" and "If you please."

Wilful waste brings woeful want
And you may live to say,
How I wish I had that crust
That once I threw away.

A child should always say what's true
And speak when he is spoken to,
And behave mannerly at table;
At least as far as he is able.

ROBERT LOUIS STEVENSON

REBECCA'S AFTER THOUGHT

Yesterday, Rebecca Mason,
  In the parlor by herself,
Broke a handsome china basin,
  Placed upon the mantel-shelf.

Quite alarmed, she thought of going
  Very quietly away,
Not a single person knowing,
  Of her being there that day.

But Rebecca recollected
  She was taught deceit to shun;
And the moment she reflected,
  Told her mother what was done;

Who commended her behavior,
Loved her better, and forgave her.

ELIZABETH TURNER

What does little birdie say
In her nest at peep of day?
Let me fly, says little birdie,
Mother, let me fly away.
Birdie, rest a little longer,
Till the little wings are stronger.
So she rests a little longer,
Then she flies away.

ALFRED TENNYSON

Sing a song of sixpence,
  A pocket full of rye;
Four-and-twenty blackbirds
  Baked in a pie;

When the pie was opened,
  The birds began to sing:
Wasn't that a dainty dish
  To set before the King?

The King was in his counting-house
  Counting out his money;
The Queen was in the parlor
  Eating bread and honey;
The maid was in the garden
  Hanging out the clothes,
When down came a blackbird,
  And nipped off her nose.

35

WYNKEN, BLYNKEN, AND NOD

Wynken, Blynken, and Nod one night
   Sailed off in a wooden shoe,—
Sailed on a river of crystal light
   Into a sea of dew.
"Where are you going, and what do you
      wish?"
   The old moon asked the three.
"We have come to fish for the herring fish
   That live in this beautiful sea;
   Nets of silver and gold have we!"
     Said Wynken,
     Blynken,
     And Nod.

The old moon laughed and sang a song,
   As they rocked in the wooden shoe;
And the wind that sped them all night long
   Ruffled the waves of dew.
The little stars were the herring fish
   That lived in that beautiful sea—
"Now cast your nets wherever you wish,—
   Never afeard are we!"
   So cried the stars to the fishermen three,
     Wynken,
     Blynken,
     And Nod.

All night long their nets they threw
    To the stars in the twinkling foam,—
Then down from the skies came the wooden
        shoe,
    Bringing the fishermen home:
'Twas all so pretty a sail, it seemed
    As if it could not be;
And some folk thought 'twas a dream they'd
        dreamed
    Of sailing that beautiful sea;
    But I shall name you the fishermen three:
        Wynken,
        Blynken,
        And Nod.

Wynken and Blynken are two little eyes,
    And Nod is a little head,
And the wooden shoe that sailed the skies
    Is a wee one's trundle-bed;
So shut your eyes while Mother sings
    Of wonderful sights that be,
And you shall see the beautiful things
    As you rock in the misty sea
    Where the old shoe rocked the fishermen
        three:—
        Wynken,
        Blynken,
        And Nod.

EUGENE FIELD

When children are playing alone on the green,
In comes the playmate that never was seen.
When children are happy and lonely and good,
The Friend of the Children comes out of the
wood.

ROBERT LOUIS STEVENSON

Gertrude Jeykell's Fairy Cakes

A*s many of you know, Gertrude Jeykell was an artist and a skilled embroiderer before she turned fully to gardening. In her book,* Children and Gardens, *she displays a culinary talent as well. I've adapted her recipe for Fairy Cakes. It is simple to make, tastes a little like a scone, and is perfect for breakfast or snacks.*

1 CUP FLOUR	½ CUP SUGAR
1 TEASPOON BAKING POWDER	½ CUP RAISINS
½ CUP UNSALTED BUTTER	1 EGG
	½ CUP MILK

✦ Preheat oven to 350° F. and grease a 9-inch square cake pan.

✦ Mix the flour and baking powder in a bowl.

✦ Cream the butter and blend it into the flour mixture.

✦ Add the sugar and raisins.

✦ Beat the egg and milk together and add to mixture. Blend lightly and spoon into pan.

✦ Bake 25 minutes. Let cool, remove from tin and cut into squares.

MAKES ABOUT 20 SMALL SQUARES

Little children, never give
Pain to things that feel and live;
Let the gentle robin come
For the crumbs you save at home,—
As his meat you throw along
He'll repay you with a song;
Never hurt the timid hare
Peeping from her green grass lair,
Let her come and sport and play
On the lawn at close of day;
The little lark goes soaring high
To the bright windows of the sky,
Singing as if 'twere always spring,
And fluttering on an untired wing,—
Oh! let him sing his happy song,
Nor do these gentle creatures wrong.

Go to bed late,
Stay very small;
Go to bed early,
Grow very tall.

One thing at a time
    And that done well,
Is a very good rule,
    As many can tell.

One, two, whatever you do,
Start it well and carry it through.
Try, try, never say die,
things will come right,
    You know, by and by.

Cock crows in the morning to tell us to rise,
And he who lies late will never be wise;
For early to bed and early to rise
Is the way to be healthy and wealthy and wise.

Simple Simon met a pieman
  Going to the fair;
Says Simple Simon to the pieman,
  "Let me taste your ware."

WHAT CAN THE MATTER BE?

O dear, what can the matter be?
Dear, dear, what can the matter be?
O dear, what can the matter be?
Johnny's so long at the fair.

He promised he'd buy me a fairing should
    please me,
And then for a kiss, oh! he vowed he would
    tease me,
He promised he'd bring me a bunch of blue
    ribbons
To tie up my bonny brown hair.

And it's O dear, what can the matter be?
Dear, dear, what can the matter be?
O dear, what can the matter be?
Johnny's so long at the fair.

MY SHADOW

I *have a little shadow that goes in and out with
    me.
And what can be the use of him is more than I
    can see.
He is very, very like me from the heels up to the
    head;
And I see him jump before me, when I jump
    into my bed.*

*The funniest thing about him is the way he
    likes to grow—
Not at all like proper children, which is always
    very slow;
For he sometimes shoots up taller, like an
    india-rubber ball,
and he sometimes gets so little that there's
    none of him at all.*

*He hasn't got a notion of how children ought to
    play,
And can only make a fool of me in every sort of
    way.
He stays so close beside me, he's a coward you
    can see;
I'd think shame to stick to nursie as that
    shadow sticks to me!*

44

One morning, very early, before the sun was
    up,
I rose and found the shining dew on every
    buttercup;
But my lazy little shadow, like an arrant
    sleepy-head,
Had stayed at home behind me and was fast
    asleep in bed.

ROBERT LOUIS STEVENSON

Pray little sheep, may I pluck as I pass
The dear little flowers that grow in the grass?
Do you think that there still will be plenty to
    eat?
I'll try not to trample the grass with my feet."

"My dear," said the sheep, "you may pluck as
    you pass,
The dear little flowers that grow in the grass;
We think there will still be sufficient to eat,
And as for the fear of your dear little feet,
They'll certainly make us the meadow more
    sweet."

45

I had a little hobby horse, it was well shod,
It carried me to London, niddety nod,
And when we got to London we heard a
    great shout,
Down fell my hobby horse and I cried out:
Up again, hobby horse, if thou be a beast,
When we get to our town we will have a feast,
And if there be but little, why thou shalt
    have some,
And dance to the bag-pipes and beating
    of the drum.

Mom's Gingersnaps

Gingersnaps seem to have gone out of fashion. But when we were little, my mom's were an after-school treat. We'd sit at the kitchen table, our feet almost touching the floor, slowly chewing these little cookies. Washed down with an ice-cold glass of milk, they seemed then like pure contentment.

1 CUP BUTTER	1½ TEASPOONS BAKING SODA
2 CUPS SUGAR	
2 EGGS, BEATEN	3 TEASPOONS GINGER
½ CUP MOLASSES	1 TEASPOON CINNAMON
2 TEASPOONS VINEGAR	¼ TEASPOON CLOVES
4 CUPS FLOUR	

✦ Preheat oven to 325° F. Grease several cookie sheets.

✦ Using an electric mixer, cream the butter and sugar. Add the eggs, molasses, and vinegar.

✦ Sift together the flour, baking soda, ginger, cinnamon, and cloves. Add to the mixture and blend well.

✦ Form dough into little balls about 1-inch round and place 1 inch apart on cookie sheet.

✦ Bake about 12 to 15 minutes. Remove from oven and cool.

MAKES ABOUT 75 TO 80 COOKIES

ANIMAL CRACKERS

Animal crackers, and cocoa to drink,
That is the finest of suppers, I think;
When I'm grown up and can have what I
    please
I think I shall always insist upon these.

What do you choose when you're offered a
    treat?
When Mother says, "What would you like
    best to eat?"
Is it waffles and syrup, or cinnamon toast?
It's cocoa and animal crackers that I love
    most!

The kitchen's the cosiest place that I know:
The kettle is singing, the stove is aglow,
And there in the twilight, how jolly to see
The cocoa and animals waiting for me.

Daddy and Mother dine later in state,
With Mary to cook for them, Susan to wait;
But they don't have nearly as much fun as I
Who eats in the kitchen with Nurse standing
    by;
and Daddy once said, he would like to be me
Having cocoa and animals once more for tea!

CHRISTOPHER MORLEY

MY DOG

His nose is short and scrubby;
    His ears hang rather low;
And he always brings the stick back,
    No matter how far you throw.

He gets spanked rather often
    For things he shouldn't do,
Like lying-on-beds, and barking,
    And eating up shoes when they're new.

He always wants to be going
    Where he isn't supposed to go.
He tracks up the house when it's snowing—
    Oh, puppy, I love you so.

MARCHETTE CHUTE

How doth the little busy bee
    Improve each shining hour
And gather honey all the day
    From every passing flower!

ISAAC WATTS

Swing, swing, sing, sing,
Here! my throne and I am king!
Swing, sing, swing, sing,
Farewell, earth, for I'm on the wing!

WILLIAM ALLINGHAM

PLAYGROUNDS

In summer I am very glad
  We children are so small,
For we can see a thousand things
  That men can't see at all.

They don't know much about the moss
  And all the stones they pass:
They never lie and play among
  The forests in the grass:

They walk about a long way off;
  And, when we're at the sea,
Let father stoop as best he can
  He can't find things like me.

But, when the snow is on the ground
  And all the puddles freeze,
I wish that I were very tall,
  High up above the trees.

LAURENCE ALMA-TADEMA

A CHILD'S PRAYER

Make me, dear Lord, polite and kind
    To every one, I pray.
And may I ask you how you find
    Yourself, dear Lord, to-day?

JOHN BANISTER TABB

THE NEW BABY

Nursie, what a little dear;
We are glad to have him here,
With his lovely bright blue eyes—
Such a charming sweet surprise.

How could such a tiny dear,
Ever reach the world down here?
Did he come at dead of night,
Like a little angel white?

Did he come here all alone?
Is he for our very own?
Nursie, tell us, will he stay
Here to join us in our play?

Oh! what tiny hands and feet,
Isn't he a little sweet—
We do love him very much,
Should we hurt him if we touch.
All we want to ask is this:
May we give him just one kiss.

A kiss to make it better,
　　Dear Nan," said little Nell.
"Now, no more tears, for see why here's
　　A kiss to make it well.

"If Dolly has a headache,
　　Or breaks an arm in two,
Why kiss the place to make it well,
　　That's all you have to do.

"If pussy cat should scratch you,
　　Don't cry, and scream, and yell,
You only have to kiss the place
　　And that will make it well."

How happy if we always
　　Could say like little Nell:
When any little trouble comes,
　　A kiss will make it well.

Only a baby small,
　　Dropped from the skies,
Only a laughing face,
　　Two sunny eyes;
Only two cherry lips,
　　One chubby nose;
Only two little hands,
　　Ten little toes.

MATTHIAS BARR

I am the sister of him
    And he is my brother.
He is too little for us
    To talk to each other.

So every morning I show him
    My doll and my book;
But every morning he still is
    Too little to look.

DOROTHY ALDIS

Monday's child is fair of face,
Tuesday's child is full of grace,
Wednesday's child is full of woe,
Thursday's child has far to go,
Friday's child is loving and giving,
Saturday's child works hard for its living,
And a child that is born on the Sabbath day
Is fair and wise and good and gay.

Hush-a-bye, baby,
    on the tree top,
When the wind blows
    the cradle will rock;
When the bough breaks
    the cradle will fall,
Down will come baby,
    cradle, and all.

Little baby, lay your head
On your pretty cradle-bed;
Shut your eye-peeps, now the day
And the light are gone away;
All the clothes are tucked in tight;
Little baby dear, good-night.

JANE TAYLOR

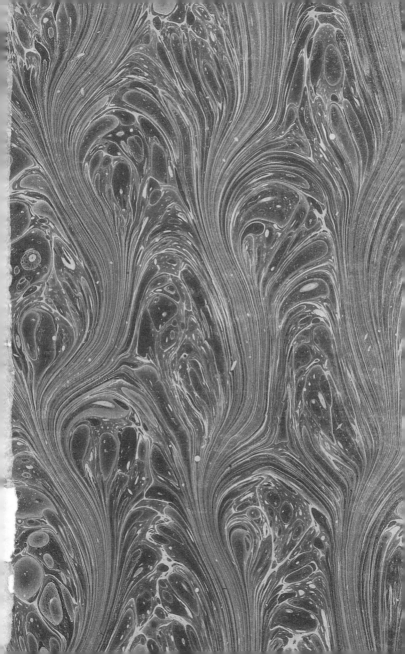

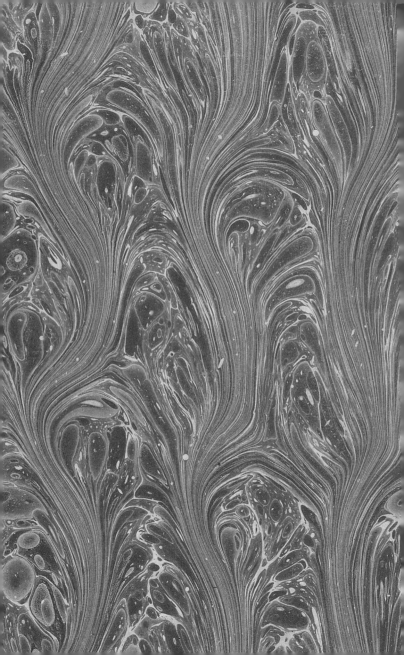